The Wright Brothers

Helen Cox Cannons

raintree

a Capstone company — publishers for children

Raintree is an imprint of Capstone Global Library Limited, a company incorporated in England and Wales having its registered office at 264 Banbury Road, Oxford, OX2 7DY – Registered company number: 6695582

www.raintree.co.uk
myorders@raintree.co.uk

Text © Capstone Global Library Limited 2016
The moral rights of the proprietor have been asserted.

Edited by Clare Lewis
Designed by Steve Mead
Picture research by Kelly Garvin
Production by Helen McCreath
Originated by Capstone Global Library
Printed and bound in China

ISBN 978 1 4747 1433 4
19 18 17 16 15
10 9 8 7 6 5 4 3 2 1

British Library Cataloguing in Publication Data
A full catalogue record for this book is available from the British Library.

Acknowledgements
We would like to thank the following for permission to reproduce images: Alamy: Chronicle, 6, INTERFOTO, 18; Glow Images: Superstock/Science Facion, 5; Library of Congress Prints and Photographs Division, 8, 10 (top), 16, 19, 21; Newscom: akg-images, 14, John T. Daniels, 17, Picture History, 7, World History Archive, 10 (bottom), , 12, , 13; Shutterstock: Davis Ross, back cover, 22, Everett Historical, cover, Senohrabek, 4; SuperStock: Dorling Kindersley/ Exactostock-4268, 9, Science and Society, 11; The Image Works: Mary Evans Picture Library, 15; Wikimedia: LOC/ Wilbur Wright, 20
Design Elements
Shutterstock: LiliGraphie, Osipovfoto

Every effort has been made to contact copyright holders of material reproduced in this book. Any omissions will be rectified in subsequent printings if notice is given to the publisher.

Contents

Some words are shown in bold, **like this.** You can
find out what they mean by looking in the glossary.

Who were the Wright brothers?

Aeroplanes are amazing. They are huge and heavy but they can fly through the air. They can take us from one country to another in a short time.

Two brothers, Wilbur and Orville Wright,
invented the aeroplane over 100 years
ago. Their aeroplane looked very different
from aeroplanes we know today.
This is the story of their invention.

What was their childhood like?

Wilbur and Orville Wright were born in 1867 and 1871. Wilbur was the third-oldest of seven children. Orville was the sixth-born child. They were raised in Dayton, Ohio, USA.

Orville Wright

Wilbur and Orville's father, Milton, was a preacher. Their parents were strict with them but very loving. The Wright children were encouraged to work hard and do well at school.

Wilbur Wright

What made them interested in flying?

Wilbur and Orville had a flying toy that their father had given them. It had a paper body. Other parts were made of cork and bamboo. A rubber band gave it power.

Wilbur and Orville's father

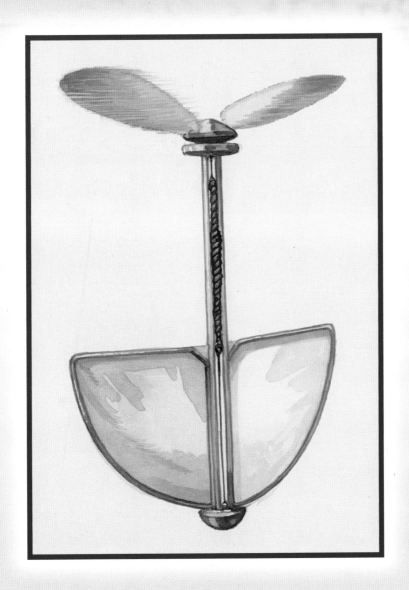

The young boys played with this toy until it broke. But they remembered what it looked like. They promised each other that one day they would fly in the air just like their toy.

What did the brothers do when they left school?

Wilbur and Orville kept their love of flight and mechanics as they got older. When they left school they started a printing business. They **invented** a new type of printing press.

In the 1890s, bicycles became very popular in the United States. So Wilbur and Orville sold their printing business and opened a bicycle shop. They called their business the Wright Cycle Company.

What was their first step towards flying?

Wilbur and Orville's interest in bicycles moved to **aviation**. A German man, Otto Lilienthal, was working on **gliders** during the 1890s. Otto's glider flights became famous. He became known as the "Glider King".

Otto died in 1896 when he fell from a glider. Orville and Wilbur knew flying was dangerous. But they wanted to build their own gliders. In 1900, after lots of attempts, Orville and Wilbur built a **manned** biplane glider.

What was the first aeroplane like?

In 1902 Wilbur and Orville realized that wind power was not enough to make their **gliders** fly for long. They began working on a "flying machine" with an engine.

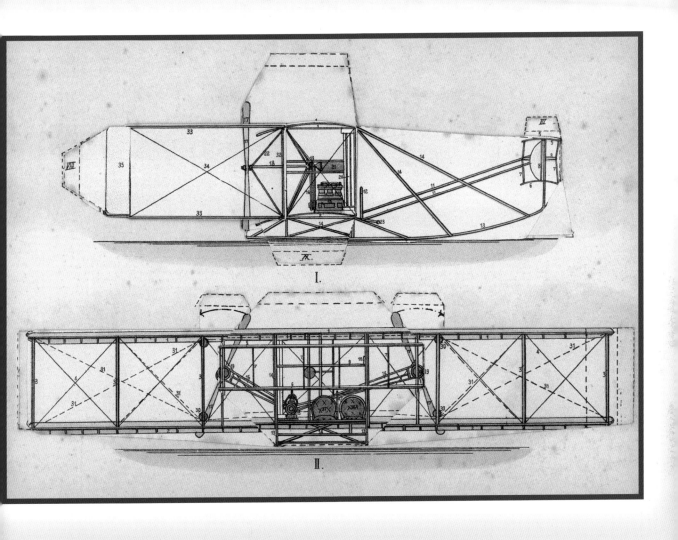

Wilbur and Orville asked their best
mechanic, Charlie Taylor, to help them.
Charlie Taylor designed a light **aluminium**
engine in just six weeks. The plane was
named The Flyer.

When and where was the first flight?

On 14 December 1903 Wilbur and Orville stood with The Flyer near Kitty Hawk, North Carolina. They tossed a coin to see who would fly it. Older brother Wilbur won the toss. But The Flyer did not fly.

Three days later, on 17 December 1903,
Orville lay in the frame of The Flyer and
it flew at last! It flew a distance of
36.5 metres (120 feet) for 12 seconds.
It was the first controlled aeroplane flight
ever made.

Why did they build The Flyer II?

On that same day, Wilbur and Orville made four flights between them. On the final flight, Wilbur flew in the air for 59 seconds. But afterwards, a sudden gust of wind damaged the plane.

The brothers carried on with their work. The next year they built a new plane, The Flyer II. On 19 September 1904, The Flyer II became the first aircraft to fly a complete circle in the air.

How did the brothers become famous?

Wilbur and Orville kept working hard on designing a better aircraft. By July 1905, Orville and Wilbur had built The Flyer III. It crashed on its first flight.

After it was **rebuilt**, The Flyer III became
the world's first practical aeroplane. It
managed to fly for 24 miles in 39 minutes.
By 1908, the Wright brothers were famous
all over the world.

How do we remember the Wright brothers?

Today, a memorial stands in the place where the Wright brothers made their first flight in The Flyer I. People all over the world remember their determination and hard work.

Aeroplanes now carry people all over the world every day. The Wright brothers would be amazed at today's aeroplanes!

Glossary

aluminium strong light metal that does not easily rust

glider light aircraft without a motor

invent to design and make something new

manned controlled by a person who is on board

mechanic person who works with tools, machines and motors

rebuild build again

Find out more

The Wright Brothers, Andrew Santella (The Child's World, 2014)

Who Were the Wright Brothers?, Jim Buckley (G P Putnam's Sons, 2014)

Index